DISCOVER THE OCEANS

Southern Ocean

by Emily Rose Oachs

BLASTOFF!
3
READERS

BELLWETHER MEDIA · MINNEAPOLIS, MN

Note to Librarians, Teachers, and Parents:

Blastoff! Readers are carefully developed by literacy experts and combine standards-based content with developmentally appropriate text.

Level 1 provides the most support through repetition of high-frequency words, light text, predictable sentence patterns, and strong visual support.

Level 2 offers early readers a bit more challenge through varied simple sentences, increased text load, and less repetition of high-frequency words.

Level 3 advances early-fluent readers toward fluency through increased text and concept load, less reliance on visuals, longer sentences, and more literary language.

Level 4 builds reading stamina by providing more text per page, increased use of punctuation, greater variation in sentence patterns, and increasingly challenging vocabulary.

Level 5 encourages children to move from "learning to read" to "reading to learn" by providing even more text, varied writing styles, and less familiar topics.

Whichever book is right for your reader, Blastoff! Readers are the perfect books to build confidence and encourage a love of reading that will last a lifetime!

This edition first published in 2016 by Bellwether Media, Inc.

No part of this publication may be reproduced in whole or in part without written permission of the publisher. For information regarding permission, write to Bellwether Media, Inc., Attention: Permissions Department, 5357 Penn Avenue South, Minneapolis, MN 55419.

Library of Congress Cataloging-in-Publication Data

Oachs, Emily Rose.
    Southern Ocean / by Emily Rose Oachs.
      pages cm. – (Blastoff! Readers: Discover the Oceans)
    Includes bibliographical references and index.
    Summary: "Simple text and full-color photography introduce beginning readers to the Southern Ocean. Developed by literacy experts for students in kindergarten through third grade"– Provided by publisher.
    Audience: Ages 5-8.
    Audience: K to grade 3.
    ISBN 978-1-62617-334-7 (hardcover : alk. paper)
    1. Antarctic Ocean–Juvenile literature. I. Title.
    GC461.O34 2016
    910.9167–dc23
                        2015033444

Table of Contents

The Newest Ocean

The Southern Ocean was named a world ocean in 2000. Before then, there were only four **recognized** oceans.

In 1914, Ernest Shackleton wanted to explore the **South Pole**. He set sail for Antarctica. But the Southern Ocean's ice crushed his ship!

DID YOU KNOW?

O Some people call the Southern Ocean the Antarctic Ocean or the South Polar Ocean.

O In 2014, an iceberg from Antarctica floated into the open Southern Ocean. It was more than 20 miles (32 kilometers) long!

O Parts of the Southern Ocean never see the sun in June and July. In December and January, the sun always shines!

O Albatrosses often fly over rough Antarctic waters. Their wings can measure 11 feet (3.4 meters) from tip to tip!

Where Is the Southern Ocean?

The Pacific, Atlantic, and Indian Oceans meet at the Southern Ocean. The ocean sits in the Western, Eastern, and Southern **hemispheres**.

The Southern Ocean touches only one **continent**. Its waters surround Antarctica. The ocean flows into the Weddell and Ross Seas.

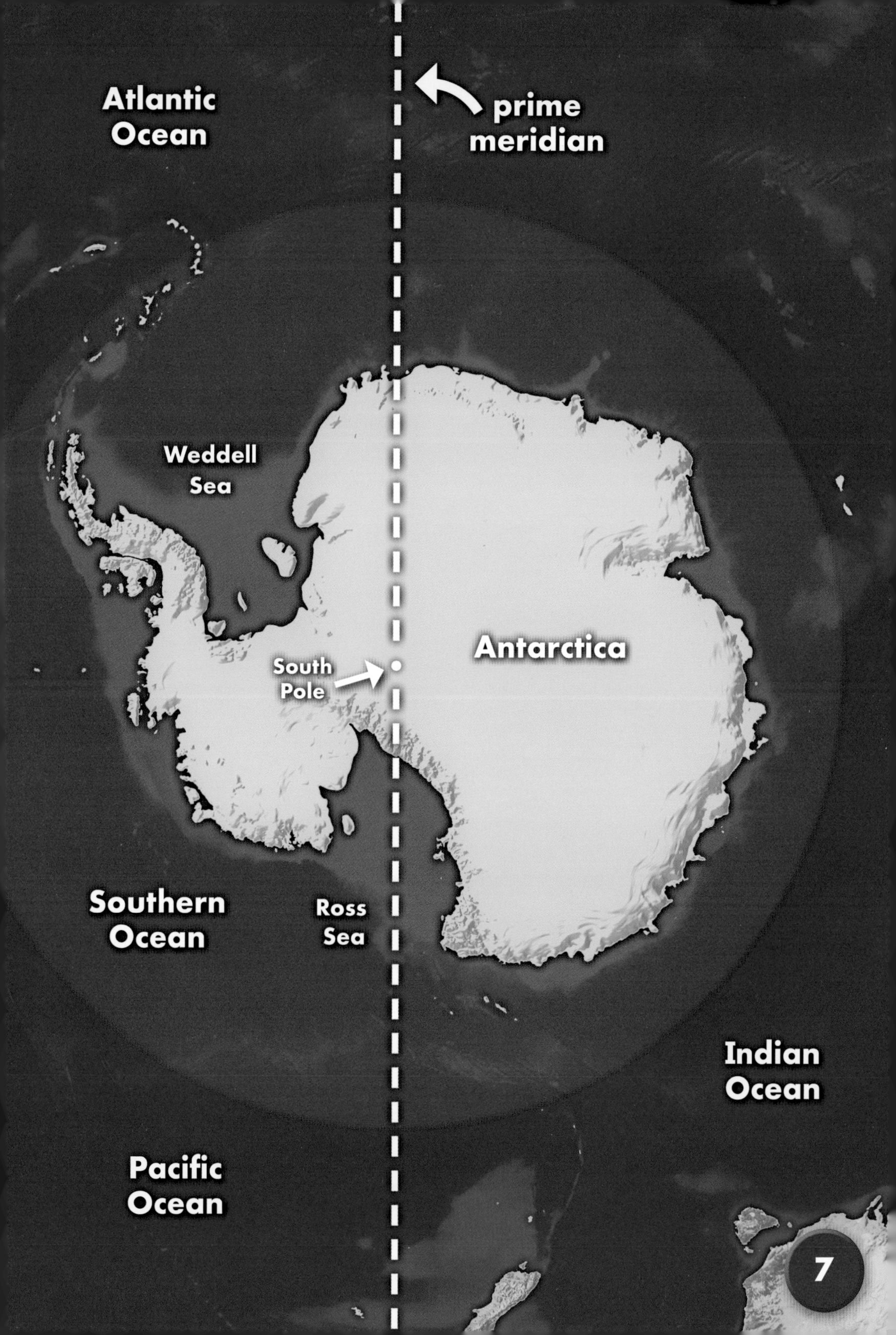

Atlantic
Ocean

prime
meridian

Weddell
Sea

Antarctica

South
Pole

Southern
Ocean

Ross
Sea

Indian
Ocean

Pacific
Ocean

The Climate and Features

Huge waves and strong winds are common in the Southern Ocean. Swirling storms sometimes form over the water.

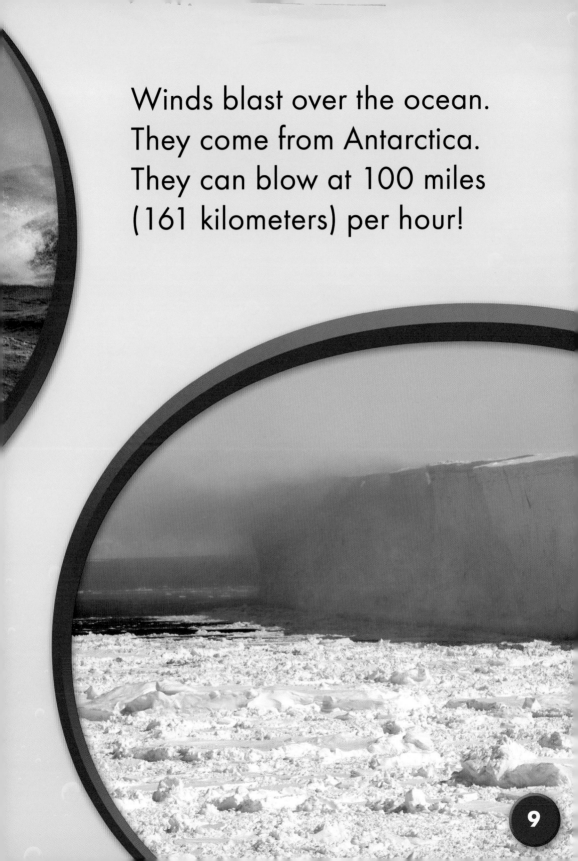

Winds blast over the ocean.
They come from Antarctica.
They can blow at 100 miles
(161 kilometers) per hour!

ice shelves

During winter, much of the ocean's surface **freezes**. Some of the ice melts in the summer sun.

Ice shelves connect to Antarctica's coast. They float on the Southern Ocean. Sometimes, chunks of ice break off. These become **icebergs**.

iceberg

Polar Front

A natural border separates the Southern Ocean from the Atlantic, Pacific, and Indian oceans.

This is called a **polar front**. The border changes as water moves.

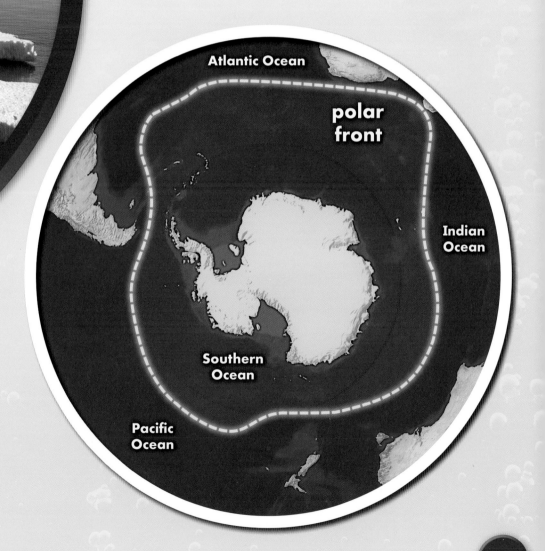

Atlantic Ocean

polar front

Indian Ocean

Southern Ocean

Pacific Ocean

Cold Antarctic waters and warmer waters from the other oceans meet at the polar front. Many ocean creatures live there.

lantern fish

Sea birds and krill are found near the surface. Lantern fish glow in the polar front's deep, dark waters.

The Plants and Animals

Few plants survive in the Southern Ocean's cold water. But **phytoplankton** grow quickly during summer months.

Phytoplankton are important to the Southern Ocean's **food chain**. Krill eat phytoplankton. Blue whales and squid feast on krill.

blue whale eating krill

krill

phytoplankton

Seals dive deep below the ice. They hunt and hide from orcas. Both of these **mammals** have **blubber** to stay warm.

orca

seal

penguin

Penguins' thick feathers let them swim through the cold ocean. Animals in the Southern Ocean are built to survive its icy waters!

Fast Facts About the Southern Ocean

Size: 7.8 million square miles (20.3 million square kilometers); 2nd smallest ocean

Average Depth: 14,764 feet (4,500 meters)

Greatest Depth: 23,737 feet (7,235 meters)

Major Bodies of Water: Amundsen Sea, Bellingshausen Sea, Weddell Sea, Ross Sea

Continent Touched: Antarctica

Total Coastline: 11,165 miles (17,968 kilometers)

Top Natural Resources: freshwater icebergs, squid, whales, krill

Famous Shipwrecks:
- *Antarctic* (1903)
- *Endurance* (1915)

Endurance

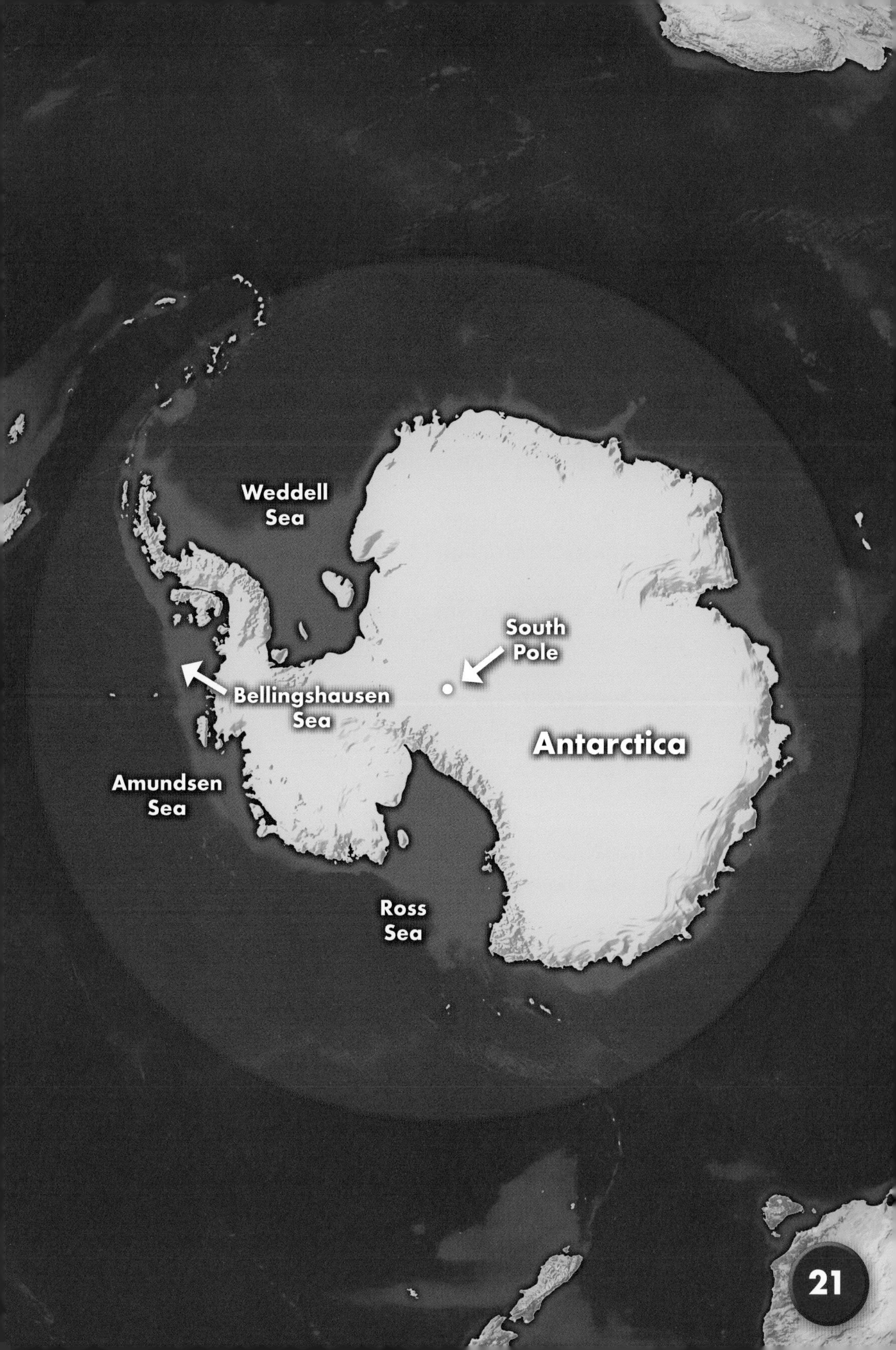

Weddell
Sea

South
Pole

Bellingshausen
Sea

Antarctica

Amundsen
Sea

Ross
Sea

Glossary

blubber—a thick layer of fat under the skin of some ocean mammals

continent—one of the seven main land areas on Earth; the continents are Africa, Antarctica, Asia, Australia, Europe, North America, and South America.

food chain—a system of who eats what

freezes—to turn water into ice; the temperature must be 28 degrees Fahrenheit (-2 degrees Celsius) for salt water.

hemispheres—halves of the globe; the equator and prime meridian divide Earth into different hemispheres.

ice shelves—huge sheets of floating ice that are connected to land

icebergs—large pieces of floating ice in the ocean

mammals—warm-blooded animals that have backbones and feed their young milk

phytoplankton—tiny ocean plants that drift

polar front—an imaginary line where cold waters meet warm waters; the polar front in the Southern Ocean is also called the Antarctic Convergence.

recognized—to agree something exists

South Pole—Earth's southernmost point

To Learn More

AT THE LIBRARY

Desmond, Jenni. *The Blue Whale*. New York, N.Y.: Enchanted Lion Books, 2015.

Meinking, Mary. *Who Counts the Penguins? Working in Antarctica*. Chicago, Ill.: Raintree, 2011.

Spilsbury, Louise and Richard. *Southern Ocean*. Chicago, Ill.: Heinemann Raintree, 2015.

ON THE WEB

Learning more about the Southern Ocean is as easy as 1, 2, 3.

1. Go to www.factsurfer.com.

2. Enter "Southern Ocean" into the search box.

3. Click the "Surf" button and you will see a list of related web sites.

With factsurfer.com, finding more information is just a click away.

Index

The images in this book are reproduced through the courtesy of: Steve Jones/ Stocktrek Images/ Corbis, front cover (left); Paul Souders/ Corbis, front cover (right); MarcAndreLeTourneux, p. 4; Janelle Lugge, p. 5; Michael S. Nolan/ Age Fotostock, p. 8; Wolfgang Kaehler/ Getty Images, p. 9; Russell Millner/ Alamy, p. 10; Bernhard Staehli, p. 11; axily, p. 12; feathercollector, pp. 14-15; Oceanwide Images.com, p. 15 (bottom); SeaPics.com, Inc., pp. 16-17; Dmytro Pylypenko, pp. 17 (top right), 18 (right); Micro Discovery/ Corbis, p. 17 (bottom right); Monika Wieland, p. 18 (left); ChameleonsEye, p. 19; Corbis/ Underwood & Underwood, p. 20.